Race Traps.

by

Tamara Williams

Printed in the United States of America

First Printing, 2015

ISBN-13: 978-0692347508

Moving Spirits, Inc.
Brooklyn, NY

www.movingspirits.org

Race Traps

A deeper Over-Standing of systematized oppression in the United States of America.

Text by Tamara Williams

Moving Spirits, Inc.

Acknowledgements

I offer my deepest gratitude to my sister, Tijwanna Ketter, for her never-ending support of my passions in life. I honor my mother and father, Daniel and Ira Williams, for their love and providing me with the solid foundation in which I stand. I wish to thank Ida Shannon, Julia Green, Eugene Ketter, and the Williams Family for their continued interest in my endeavors and ideas.

I give many thanks to Lennell Shackleford for his honest feedback and encouragement. I am grateful for the members of Moving Spirits, Inc. and all that they have offered to the vision the organization. I give thanks to Baba Sekou Alaje and Ogbe Soto for the abundance of wisdom shared with me in life.

I pay homage to my ancestors for paving the way and providing me with great strength through my journeys.

Table of Contents

Subservient mentality in the United States has been our detriment.

After the verdict for Mike Brown someone invited me to a healing circle.

Fuck healing.
I don't need to be healed right now.
What I need is resolution AND action.
Justice.

Save that healing shit for someone else. I don't need healing, not in the same way that my brothers living in the system do. Not in the same way as my brothers and sisters incarcerated inside and outside of the prisons do. Not in the same way that my family in the projects need it. They need our help, before they need our healing. Or perhaps we can give that simultaneously. We need Justice; we need to be treated like human beings.

We Need to stop hanging around in our living rooms talking and discussing and MOVE.
We Need a movement.

Let me be transparent in saying to many, don't act as though you live the same kind of life as some of our brothers. You don't. And they know you don't. I am not afraid to say I'm privileged: Privileged enough to know about resources, to even know where to begin to look for them, privileged in my education, to even write this text.

Let's start with awareness and acknowledgements, of where each of us stands. We have to be the ones that provide for our brothers, sisters and children that have been infiltrated as prey to our nation's systems. How can we expect the same systems designed to castrate and degenerate us, to help us?

So fuck healing.

Healing starts when we wake up and start helping each other; rich and poor. We must assist each other, not only in spirit, but in the monetary value that this society decides to strip away from us each day.

Gentrification anyone?

Society knows the power of black bodies living together.
That is why they'd rather break us apart and forcibly push us out of
our OWN   neighborHoods.

Black Wall Street?
Ever read about this in your history books?
No surprise if this is your introduction.
The society that we live in, only wants us to live in bondage under
their degrading rules and employment. This is the entire premise of
the projects being constructed in the 1960s. Take black families,
separate the male from his seeds and wife, provide

                                    neighborHoods

                        with
                the worst education possible,
                    the deadliest foods,
            mass manufactured drugs and guns

Bring them into these

                                    neighborHoods

and provide a monthly
check
so there's just enough for families to survive.

Not survive on

knowledge,

food

or community.

Survive long enough or until one of these things kills him- lack of
education which leads to

sickness,

drugs,

poor health.

Or let them survive until lack of community kills them through

gun violence,

self hate

and destroyed families.

Let's not be fooled by the media's part in this. What do you see
when you turn on the majority of Black movies?
Buffoonery.
What is in black reality shows?
Blacks hungry for money and fame. What do you see on the news?
Blacks killing each other.

Make no mistake.   This is no coincidence.

Wake up.

Media

The media is NOT showing any coverage of the protests happening in (Y)OUR STREETS. But had North Korea, the Sony hacking and the drama of *The Interview* in your face All last week!

And what happened to Ebola?
Hmmm???

If you don't get it by now, WAKE UP!!!

We have become desensitised to violence against black men, women and children worldwide.

What it is

"It" is a matter of systematized racism that has been formed since the beginning of this country. Sadly, it IS a matter of black and white because it is a justice system that is designed not to bring Justice to blacks.... Mass incarceration anyone? We are fighting a race battle in a country in which quite frankly, black people were never meant to be

free.

That is the issue. That is why people are angry. We've gone through years of genocide, in this country and so many others, and these verdicts (Trayvon Martin, Mike Brown, Eric Garner and countless others) are just reassurance that people just don't "get it". And rather turn a blind eye. Like any issue, a solution cannot be determined until we ALL look into the root of the problem face to face.

The only thought that I keep having today:

Racism and mistreatment of blacks is rampant Worldwide, not nationwide.
And this thought just put some things in perspective for me.
12/4/2014

Dear Black People,

Please be careful and mindful of the power that you hold. Use your minds as much as your talents. Nicki Minaj is republican... what the hell for? So she can help take away from those that have supported her career? To make it virtually impossible for those she's left behind to succeed? People please use your fame & influence to advocate and support those that don't have a voice for themselves.

This is critical to the Inner-standing that Black Lives Matter[1].

Dear Black People,

Right now is the perfect time to sit down with someone that you love, and talk to them about Our crisis. How we must value black lives. And why it is absolutely necessary for all black people to not only feel repulsed when the government systematically kills us, but when we kill each other.
Accountability, Community, Responsibility begins.

Because, Black Lives Matter[1].

Large Corporations and Businesses

Stop giving money to companies that fund the politicians, who create the laws which are used by law enforcement (and other systems) to oppress black people.

Stop giving money to companies that take money from the black community. Support each other, buy locally (if the money stays in your neighbourhood) and support independently owned black businesses.

History has taught us about the mass bargaining and purchasing of slaves, which is something to reflect upon as a country based on capitalism and wealth developed by the strenuous work of others.

KNOW what your money is going to support when it leaves your pockets! Why is this bad? You may question. This does nothing more than further facilitate a system of mass incarceration, for mass production for mass consumerism.

Take a deeper look into what our nation is facilitating.

"Prison labor in the United States is referred to as insourcing. Under the Work Opportunity Tax Credit (WOTC), employers receive a tax credit of $2,400 for every work-release inmate they employ as a reward for hiring 'risky target groups.'

The workers are not only cheap labor, but they are considered easier to control. They also tend to be African-American males. Companies are free to avoid providing benefits like health insurance or sick days. They also don't need to worry about unions, demands for vacation time, raises or family issues.

With all of that productivity, the inmates make about 90 cents to $4 a day.

Here are some of the biggest corporations to use such practices, but there are hundreds more:

1. McDonald's uses inmates to produce frozen foods. Inmates process beef for patties. They may also process bread, milk and chicken products.

2. Wendy's has also been identified as relying on prison labor to reduce its cost of operations. Inmates also process beef for patties.

3. Wal-Mart uses inmates for manufacturing purposes. The company "hires" inmates to clean products of UPC bar codes so that products can be resold.

4. Starbucks uses inmates to cut costs as well. Starbucks subcontractor Signature Packaging Solutions hired Washington state prisoners to package holiday coffees.

5. At Sprint, Inmates provide telecommunication services. Inmates are used in call centers.

6. At Verizon, Inmates provide telecommunication services.

7. Victoria's Secret uses inmates to cut production costs. In South Carolina, female inmates were used to sew products. Also, inmates reportedly have been used to replace "made in" tags with "Made in USA" tags.

8. Fidelity Investments- 401(K) or other investments are held by Fidelity, and, in some cases, some of your money invested by Fidelity is used for prison labor or in other operations related to the prison industrial complex. The investment firm funds the American Legislative Exchange Council (ALEC), which has created laws authorizing and increasing the use of inmates in manufacturing.

9. Kmart and J.C. Penney both sell jeans made by inmates in Tennessee prisons.

10. American Airlines and the car rental company Avis use inmates to take reservations." [2]

Source for pages 10-13:

Riley, Ricky. "12 Mainstream Corporations Benefiting from the Prison Industrial Complex." *Atlanta Black Star*. December 5, 2014. http://atlantablackstar.com/2014/10/10/12-mainstream-corporations-benefiting-from-the-prison-industrial-complex/.

Think about it the next time you consider major retail shopping.

This is how it is all connected to slavery and systematic oppression. I urge my brothers and sisters to continue researching the topics of mass incarceration, police brutality and systematic oppression. This information will be enlightening.

If we want to know more we have to be willing to do the work to receive it. Knowledge is power, but wisdom can be life-changing.

See how it is ALL connected?

Responsibility

Wondering why I don't see more of my friends at these protests.

Wondering why I don't hear any news of protests in Augusta, GA.

Wondering a lot right now....

I'm baffled by the fact that people are not willing to make sacrifice for change. We complain of oppression and bow down to the same system of oppression so that our lives are not inconvenienced. I'm glad our ancestors were willing to make the sacrifices that WE have benefited from today. Now it is our time to make Sacrifice for our children and that indeed only comes with risks.

Volunteering is not sacrifice, neither is grassroots activism of discussion. Signing a petition is not a sacrifice, unless you've started it, perhaps.

Lobbying, litigation, selective purchase ordinances, demonstrations, and money wrenching are. But I have only talked to a handful of people doing that.

In saying sacrifice, I mean surrendering or giving up something... other than time and money for change (or the willingness to).

If you know of other actions that are along these lines please share with others.

So, perhaps the question should be: why aren't more friends willing to make Sacrifice? If the answer is freedom, to each his own.... But then my question is, then, do we really expect change?

I am wondering because there is Strength in numbers and a fight against systematic oppression cannot be fought alone. I am not talking about broadcasting on social media, what I have been very vocal about is community and battling together. I am not asking why I don't see people on Facebook; I am asking why don't I see my friends in the streets?

In these instances, actions of others are vital if we are serious about dismantling a system. So now here comes the difficult question of who is ready to make sacrifices and sacrifices of what. What does community want to actively do together? Or has our persecution become so bad that we cannot come together? Whether it is that people come together to decide who is going to be on the battlefield and who is going to be in the background, UNITY is key. I must say, no WAR can be fought without being in the face of those you are fighting against. Again, we have to meet face to face at some point.

So the question remains,

What sacrifices are people willing to make? Or are there none?

Sacrifice is not relative when it comes to THIS issue (for me). There is a time for calm waters and there is a time for fire. Let us not forget; Osun (the Divine Spirit force from ancient African traditions) is guardian of fresh water and also a Warrior. All elements possess the capacity to be forceful and powerful as they possess sweet fluidity. The world is not balanced, we are in discord at all times, which is why plates moves, glaciers shift, rain falls, etc. Teaching, childcare, and healing have been taking place over the past years and I am not referring to these examples of being in life... A mother makes a sacrifice each day because children are born. I am referring to sacrifices needed for drastic changes in our country regarding race.

"People are not interested", that is not good enough for me to accept. I cannot accept that for my family. My uninterested folks are going to hear it until they dream it and it becomes a part of their reality.

In several black communities around the *United* States of America, I am surprised that not one protest, not one petition, not one scream has come from these majority Black cities in which racism is rampant.

We have to stop living in fear, by confronting our demons head on.

WE Have to **Do more**!

More Risks. More Action!!

Shut down commerce, shut down highways, shut down organizations... across the country.

Placing black people higher in the economic ladder to positions of power has clearly done nothing to help empower those that remain at the bottom.

So, someone asked me, "Why aren't poor people protesting?" It is quite despicable to think that only the middle class constitutes the movement of people in the streets.

However, I will say this. It is difficult to rally against systems in which your entire life has been created or better yet, Fabricated upon. It is BOLD to face a system that has your Mind and physical body, in some instances, imprisoned. As daring and challenging as it may be, these actions are absolutely necessary.

Suzy Kassem is credited for the quote that I live by: "doubt and fear kills more dreams than failure ever will".[3] Well, I am dreaming big, and I pray that my brothers and sisters are envisioning with me. That they see what is happening and gain the courage and power needed to continue our movement out of persecution, brutality, oppression and injustice together. I will say that word again, Together.

We need to be ready so we don't have to get ready. We have to continue our efforts until there is a complete shift in the current social justice system in place. Dismantling then restructuring is ideal. We are not asking permission. We are not ready to sit down with the powers that be until they are ready to speak our language. That is essential. We are creating havoc until we the people get peace. Radical changes call for radical and drastic measures. Sacrifice is needed. Do whatever you can to disrupt economics, MONEY; since it is the driving force of this country, only then, will people start to listen.

Money and violence is the only language that this country speaks and listens to. One thing that I strongly suggest is a violent act of financial change; changing the hands that receive Black people's money.
I am not saying that people need to be violent; again, I am saying that is what the government responds to.

I bring forth a reminder, the government that is urging people to be calm, is the same government killing its citizens and thousands of others in Iraq, Afghanistan, Syria, Pakistan, Liberia and Sierra Leone; Men, Women and Children.

I think in this instance we need to think about what in history has truly worked. We are looking at similar issues of systematized racism 59 years after Montgomery Bus Boycotts started, that December day. I think it is time we look at radical approaches, whether it be with money or other avenues, because as far as my knowledge serves, the Haitian Revolution was one of the most radical and life changing events of *The New World* and it was from that act alone that slaves in other nations began to get samples of freedom- because you and I both know that even today, many of us are not Truly Free.

Black on Black

Dec 28, 2012

Chicago has had 500 homicides this year.

                                        This has to end.

Focus on what we are   doing

                saying

                        teaching

                                showing.

Let us live by teaching harmony and respect for life and ourselves.

I have started by seeing the beauty in all that surrounds me.
For decades I've been taught that black is everything but beauty.
This philosophy exists today in many realms.

But now, we have to be CONSCIOUS, open our eyes, and see
                the **Beauty We Are Crafted In.**

The best day of your life is the one in which you decide your life is
                                your own.
                No apologies or excuses.
        No one to lean on, rely on, or blame.

The gift is yours - it is an amazing journey

And you alone are responsible for the quality of it.

This is the day your life really begins.

it is not what you are called, but what you answer to...

Guidance

Please people, READ. Reading each day can keep sickness, danger, the IRS...

All types of bad things away!

Read. The 6 o'clock news report does not give you the whole story. It won't. It is not designed to. Read. Have you wondered why the USA scared the nation with the Ebola crisis for 7 consecutive weeks, and then mentioned no more of it? Have you wondered why the only two men that died of Ebola in the United States were citizens of Africa? I have.

Have you heard about 20 year old DeAndre Joshua who was found dead in Ferguson, Missouri? Shot in the head and his body burned during the protests. Or Akai Gurley, a 28 year old man shot and killed by a police officer in the stairwell of a residential building; the officer stated that he was "startled". There is also Aiyana Stanley-Jones, a 7 year old girl that was fatally shot by law enforcement while sleeping in her home during a raid. Their stories were not plastered all over the news, and it will not be.

You would not receive this information from the news media. They have their own agenda. Be sure not to follow it, but make your own.

We cannot get all information from the news. We have to be willing to do the work, dig deeper, find additional resources, and read in order to enlighten ourselves. We must start having face-to-face conversations and discussions with others to find out where to start and where to go collectively.

Sometimes I choose to observe and not speak. So far, it has allowed me to see people for who they truly are... It doesn't take much to sift the truth. Listen...

Responding to Others

Please share YOUR knowledge. Uplift your community of brothers and sisters. When speaking to others about matters of police brutality, race and inequality, offer the following if people continue to question you:

"You can take what I've shared or continue questioning. Do not expect someone else to do all the work for you".

Here is my response to people that are saying, "Tamara you're going too far."

Perhaps, you haven't gone far enough. I have reached the point in which the first thing I think about when I wake up in the morning, every moment of my wakened life, the last thing I think about before I go to bed, and even in my dreams is the systematized racism, oppression, injustice and persecution towards our people. Yes, I've become obsessed, and I'm using it to fuel my actions.

So, I'm enraged and I wonder what it takes for others to say they've had enough. What are people willing to do for the changes required so that All Lives Matter?

Dedication

We so quickly forget about killers such as Eric Frein who actually murdered a police officer, escaped and was SAFELY captured. And since then, how many INNOCENT black lives have been lost due to police brutality???

- Aiyana Stanley-Jones, regardless of what is occurring here, I pray that you rest in power, peacefully.

- Trayvon Martin, regardless of what is occurring here, I pray that you rest in power, peacefully.

- Mike Brown, regardless of what is occurring here, I pray that you rest in power, peacefully.

- Eric Garner, regardless of what is occurring here, I pray that you rest in power, peacefully.

- Tamir Rice, regardless of what is occurring here, I pray that you rest in power, peacefully.

- Akai Gurley, regardless of what is occurring here, I pray that you rest in power, peacefully.

- Rumain Brisbon, regardless of what is occurring here, I pray that you rest peacefully.

And you ALL ascend even higher in the next realm. My prayers of strength are with your family and all other lives taken by the hand of injustice.

This situation of our nation is fuel to DO some things Differently.

To MY unborn son, your Black skin is beautiful and your African blood is powerful.

Wealth derives from your resources.

Here are a few **Resources** to dive deeper:

- *The new Jim Crow* by Michelle Alexander
- *The Mis-Education of the Negro* by Carter G. Woodson
- *Are prisons obsolete?* By Angela Davis
- *Willie Lynch letter: The Making of a Slave*
- *Grasping the Root of Divine Power* by Chief Yuya Assaan-ANU

Afterword

I have always been active on social media but since the rise of blatant misuse of power by authorities, the number of my Facebook and Twitter posts began to soar. In reflecting over the amount of information that I was posting in the digital world, I realized that I did not want these words to disappear with time- as this often happens in fast-paced, 2 dimensional realms; I want my thoughts and ideas to have a lasting impression.

As a result, this short book was developed from a collection of my posts and responses on social media. This text contains my responses to media, people and challenges to what is Black in America.

This text was born out of my Rage and Anxiety of the current state of our country, the United States of America. In writing, I began to feel relief from some of the boiling anger inside. However, healing has not occurred yet. I am certain that it will not begin until Black people are considered equal, non-threatening, Human beings in this country- living lives that do not entail daily abuse, fear, or persecution. Only then, will my healing from oppression begin.

About the Author

I come from
dirt roads and open fields
days at Sunset Villa
Drumlines
dancing feet and moving bodies

I come from
hands clapping, feet stomping and tambourines rattling
scrap iron
moccasins
and honeysuckles

I come from
blasting sounds of Curtis Mayfield and Prince

I come from
Davidson's Rainbow years
Garnet & Gold in Tallahassee
Being Deeply Rooted in Chicago
Dancing & Twirling in Philly
and the Concrete Jungle

I come from
sunny skies
gentle waves
century old buildings

I come from
Sango
Obatala
Egbe

I come from
Depression

I come from
Pride

I come from
Perseverance

Bibliography

1. #BlackLivesMatter was co-founded by Alicia Garza, Patrisse Cullors and Opal Tometi. Black Lives Matter was created by these strong spirits in response to the acquittal of George Zimmerman after his killing of 17-year old, Trayvon Martin. Pg. 9

2. Riley, Ricky. "12 Mainstream Corporations Benefiting from the Prison Industrial Complex." *Atlanta Black Star*. December 5, 2014. http://atlantablackstar.com/2014/10/10/12-mainstream-corporations-benefiting-from-the-prison-industrial-complex/. Pgs. 10-13

3. Kassem, Suzy. "Doubt Kills More Dreams Than Failure Ever Will." *Style is King blog* on *Wordpress*. December 28, 2014.http://styleisking.wordpress.com/2014/08/08/doubts-kills-more-dreams-than-failure-ever-will-suzy-kassem/. Pg.17

www.ingramcontent.com/pod-product-compliance
Lightning Source LLC
Chambersburg PA
CBHW031542040426
42445CB00010B/666